CENTERS in Minutes!

Bertie Kingore
AUTHOR

Jeffery Kingore
GRAPHIC DESIGN

Professional Associates Publishing
www.kingore.com

Centers in Minutes!

Published by
PROFESSIONAL ASSOCIATES PUBLISHING
PO Box 28056
Austin, Texas 78755-8056
Toll free phone/fax: 866-335-1460
http://www.kingore.com

Printed in the United States of America
ISBN: 0-9716233-4-1

Table of Contents

INTRODUCTION

A learning center is a physical area of the classroom organized with materials and learning experiences for specific instructional purposes. Instead of overwhelming teachers with intensive preparation, *Centers in Minutes* focuses on learning rather than interior decorating. Decorations and appealing visuals can add interest, but the emphasis is on students' learning and curriculum needs.

Centers may be year-round, such as writing, math, research, and reading and listening centers, or they may be topical and change periodically. (Combinations of both are achieved by adding topical items or tasks to year-round centers.) Centers may relate to your overarching conceptual theme or reflect specific content subjects. Centers are popu-

---

Kingore, B. (2004). *Centers in Minutes.* Austin: Professional Associates Publ.

lar with many students because they incorporate diverse ways to learn away from students' usual desks or table areas.

Some educators debate whether centers are social or learning-based. Perhaps there should be no debate as both are readily incorporated. School is a place for learning together. When more than one student is in a center, socialization is invited in the context of learning discussions rather than only as social exchanges.

Learning centers are not new to teachers, but simpler preparation techniques, successful management systems, and simple organization formats may be. Instead of labor intensive, teachers need center ideas that minimize preparation and put the students' minds and bodies in learning gear.

Centers provide the means for students to practice, apply, master, and extend the concepts and skills that they are learning in order to move them toward independence. Centers cater to individual learning styles and talents by including activities structured around different learning modalities. A well developed learning center provides students with valuable content, challenging activities, and ongoing opportunities for interaction and feedback. Provide appropriate materials in centers that enable students to explore and work independent of teacher direction.

The most productive centers involve open-ended inquiry rather than simple activities. Provide multiple content-rich activities that respond to learners' diverse profiles and interests. Centers that challenge advanced learners need to include complex, tiered activities and beyond-grade-level resources--particularly an ample variety of non-fiction materials.

THE VALUE OF CENTERS

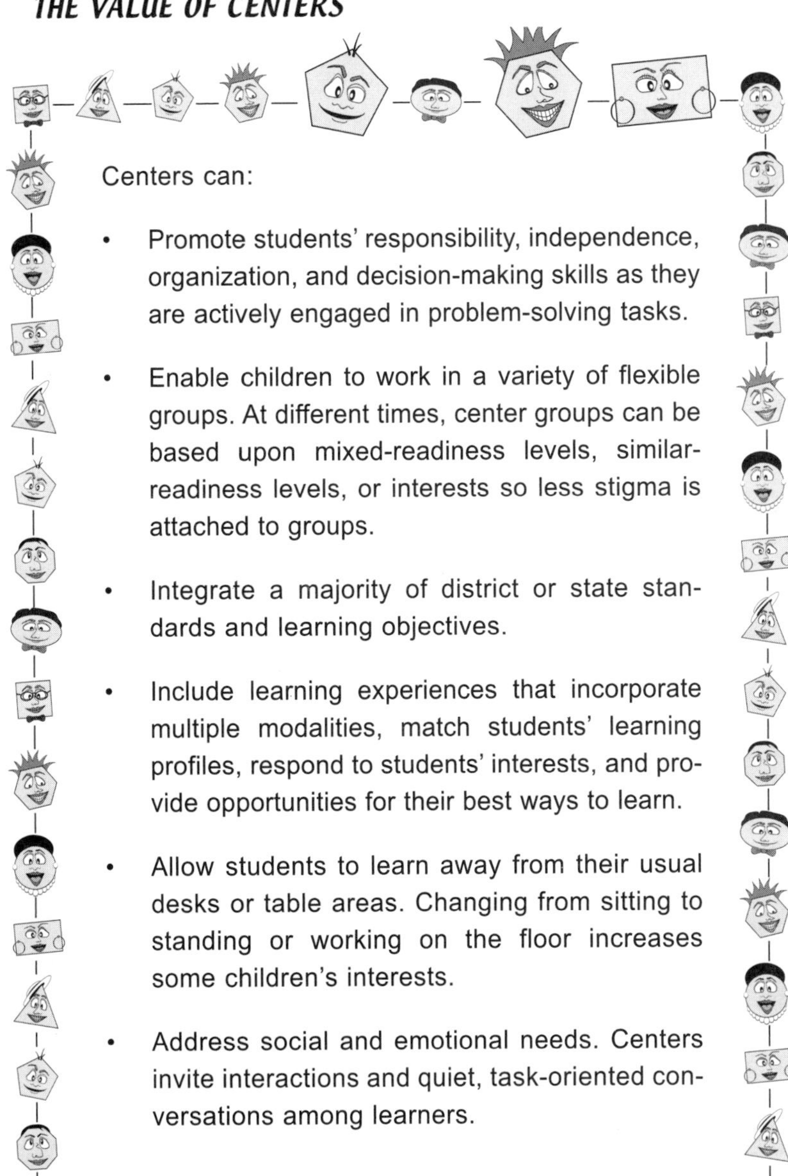

Centers can:

- Promote students' responsibility, independence, organization, and decision-making skills as they are actively engaged in problem-solving tasks.
- Enable children to work in a variety of flexible groups. At different times, center groups can be based upon mixed-readiness levels, similar-readiness levels, or interests so less stigma is attached to groups.
- Integrate a majority of district or state standards and learning objectives.
- Include learning experiences that incorporate multiple modalities, match students' learning profiles, respond to students' interests, and provide opportunities for their best ways to learn.
- Allow students to learn away from their usual desks or table areas. Changing from sitting to standing or working on the floor increases some children's interests.
- Address social and emotional needs. Centers invite interactions and quiet, task-oriented conversations among learners.

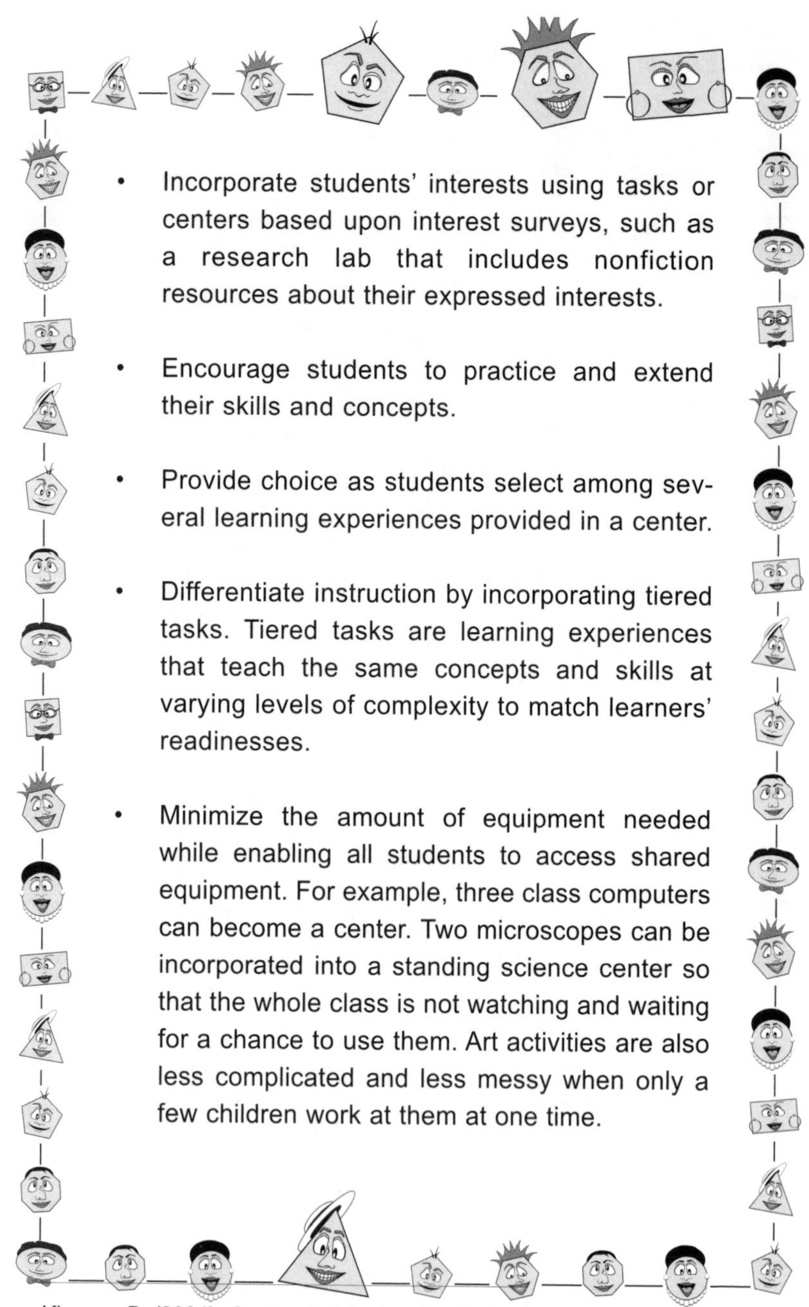

- Incorporate students' interests using tasks or centers based upon interest surveys, such as a research lab that includes nonfiction resources about their expressed interests.

- Encourage students to practice and extend their skills and concepts.

- Provide choice as students select among several learning experiences provided in a center.

- Differentiate instruction by incorporating tiered tasks. Tiered tasks are learning experiences that teach the same concepts and skills at varying levels of complexity to match learners' readinesses.

- Minimize the amount of equipment needed while enabling all students to access shared equipment. For example, three class computers can become a center. Two microscopes can be incorporated into a standing science center so that the whole class is not watching and waiting for a chance to use them. Art activities are also less complicated and less messy when only a few children work at them at one time.

QUALITY LEARNING OPPORTUNITIES

The quality of the opportunity determines the level of students' responses.

*If we fail to provide tasks that promote high-level thinking and challenge, we will have to be content with basic student responses instead of excellence.**

Why eliminate folder games and matching tasks?

During my third year of teaching, I reached a startling conclusion--I was spending three hours making a learning task for a center that students spent three minutes completing the next day! I realized that most center tasks based upon folder games or matching tasks promote simple right answers instead of thinking or problem-solving skills. Equally damaging, these simple one-answer tasks reinforce a short attention span. (I certainly did not intend for students' attention spans to be reduced to three minutes!)

I began challenging myself to think differently about center tasks.

The challenge

The challenge is to:

- Provide respectful learning experiences that are developmentally appropriate and more open-ended to encourage multiple levels of thinking and multiple correct answers.

---

*Kingore, B. (2002). *The Kingore Observation Inventory,* 2nd ed. Austin: Professional Associates Publishing.

Kingore, B. (2004). *Centers in Minutes.* Austin: Professional Associates Publ.

- Incorporate more students' products instead of adult decorations and work.

- Focus on tasks that engage young students in longer think-time but minimal writing as many children's hands wear out before their heads do.

The reward for this effort is:

- Children who are more engaged in learning are more motivated to achieve. Students feel more ownership in *their* centers. Fewer behavior problems arise when children are more meaningfully involved.

- Students take pride in posting their work so other students and visiting adults can read and respond to it. (This creates less to grade!)

- Teachers can develop centers in minutes instead of dedicating an entire summer or most weekends to producing folder games and center decorations. More complex and engaging tasks need to be changed less frequently. They capture students' interests and attention longer than simple matching or fill-in-the-blank tasks.

CREATING CENTERS

SELECTING APPROPRIATE CENTER TASKS

Choice is a powerful motivator. Some students work better when provided task choices. Rather than all children doing the same task at a center, include an appropriate number of stimulating tasks and equipment in each center to sustain the children's interests. A variety of tasks for students to select among better honors diverse learning profiles and responds to diverse readiness levels.

When there is too little to do, students often lose interest. When the choices are not stimulating or challenging, students may become bored. In both cases, behavior problems often follow. To connect centers to themes or topics, vary student choices within a center to correspond to particular contents or topics.

QUESTIONS TO ANSWER WHEN SELECTING LEARNING EXPERIENCES FOR CENTERS

- Are all of the learning experiences developmentally appropriate and matched to students' readiness levels?
- How do they actively and mentally engage students in learning?
    - How are they visually appealing and engaging for visual learners?
    - How do they incorporate bodily-kinesthetic learning?
- Are these learning tasks meaningful and authentic?
    - How are the tasks related to what students need to learn?
    - Which learning standards, concepts, and skills are integrated into the learning experiences?
- Can students successfully complete these activities without direct teacher management?
- How can the complexity of the tasks be tiered to match students' levels of readiness?
- Are the tasks designed to increase or decrease attention spans?
    - What amount of think-time is required of the students?
- How are problem solving and high-level thinking encouraged by the activity?

GUIDELINES FOR INSTRUCTIONALLY VIBRANT CENTERS

✔ Focus on important learning outcomes that are integral to the curriculum. Ensure that students are not just *doing activities*.

✔ Document standards by posting a laminated list of the learning standards which can be employed in the current center tasks. On a simple graphic, list key words of the standards for easy reference. Use a wipe-off pen to check the standards currently incorporated in the center. This process clearly signals adults and children that learning is in progress.

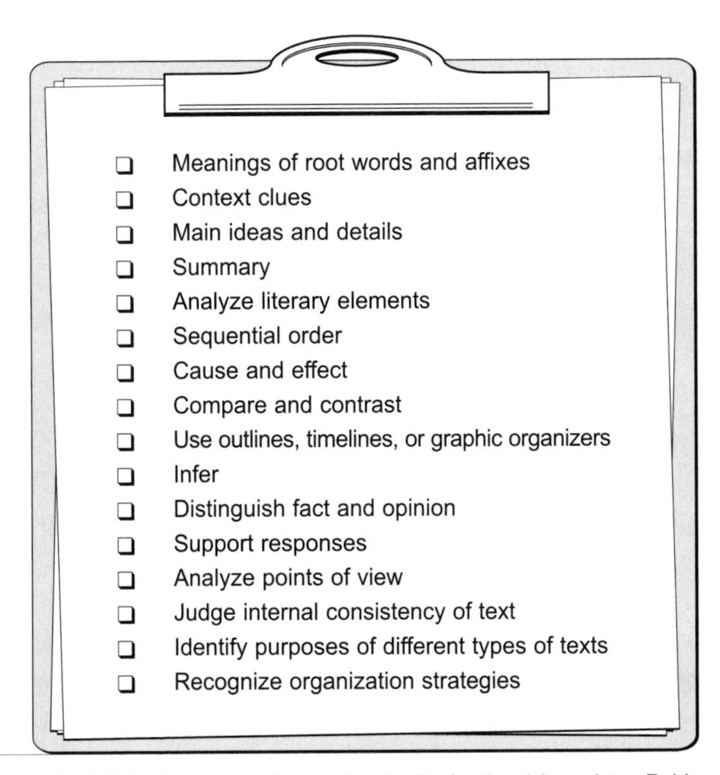

Kingore, B. (2004). *Centers in Minutes.* Austin: Professional Associates Publ.

- ✔ Promote children's high-level thinking responses instead of simple answers that respond to matching or fill-in-the-blanks tasks.

- ✔ Provide a rubric that clearly defines quality work and positive work behaviors. The rubric can be a poster on the wall or a copy in the children's centers logs. When students concretely see the preferred behaviors and levels of quality, they are more likely to work to achieve a higher level. Examples of a simple rubric for young children and a slightly expanded rubric for older students are included in the centers logs.

- ✔ Include a range of interactive activities and learning tasks that appeal to the diverse learning profiles and readiness levels of the students.

- ✔ Provide clear directions for students in centers. In some classes, it may be advisable to develop step-by-step procedures and checklists that students use to monitor their progress.

- ✔ Promote students' organization by including a cork board, boxes, in and out bins, metal rings, folders, and places for needed supplies. *A place for everything and everything in its place*.

- ✔ Develop routines for participating in centers so students understand expected behaviors, what to do, where to go, and how long to stay.

- ✔ Motivate quality responses and provide an audience for students' work in centers by including a small cork board for students to post their work. This process enables students to share their responses and products with others rather than only produce more papers for the teacher to grade.

✔ Simplify intensive preparation by creating centers in which teachers change only a few items weekly instead of developing new centers.

> ***Learning is not maximized when centers are simply convenient places to send students.***

FINDING ROOM FOR CENTERS

In a small room, space can be obtained by abolishing the idea of ownership: a desk for each child. Cluster the students' tables or desks to create centers. The desks or tables take on a multi-purpose use instead of the *one-student, one-desk, one-place* organization of the past. *Now, this is my desk for independent work. Later, this desk is part of a research lab. Then, it becomes part of a cooperative learning group task.*

Kingore, B. (2004). *Centers in Minutes.* Austin: Professional Associates Publ.

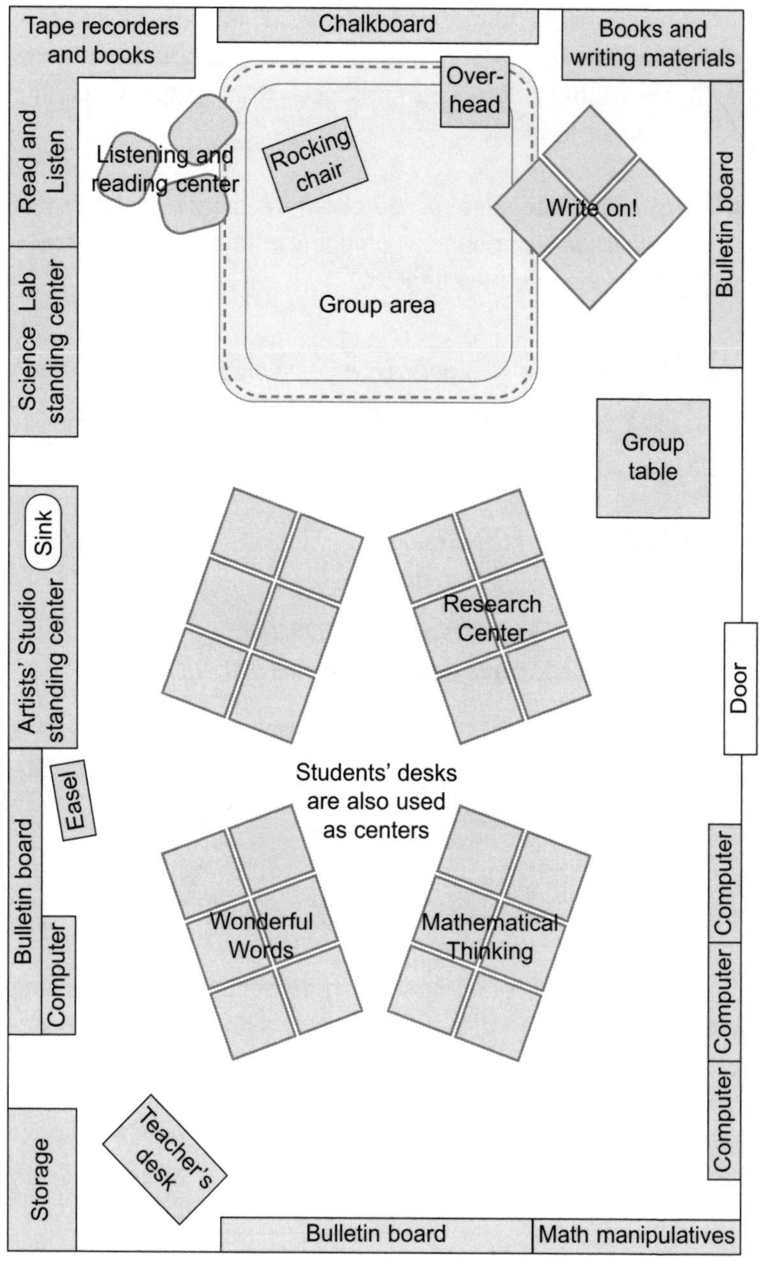

Kingore, B. (2004). *Centers in Minutes.* Austin: Professional Associates Publ.

Consider the following details when determining the location of centers.

a. Noise and activity level of centers
b. Location and availability of equipment, such as a sink, electrical outlets, and chalkboard
c. Features such as windows, doors, and storage areas
d. Traffic patterns within the room
e. Space available in different areas of the room
f. Teacher's view (Avoid placing centers where the teacher's view is obstructed.)

STANDING CENTERS

Use counter tops and extended windowsill areas as standing centers. Activities are placed along the area, and children stand to complete the tasks.

CORNER CENTERS

Add pillows and clipboards to a corner area to make a small center. An area rug adds to the visual interest of this center. A corner center is a great choice for games and manipulatives that work well on the floor.

BULLETIN BOARD CENTERS

Interactive bulletin boards can become a center. A bulletin board divided in half with yarn becomes a category center. For example, the heading of one side would read: *Magnets attract these;* and the other would be: *Magnets do not attract these.* Children use push pins or self-sticking clips to appropriately categorize pictures and small items.

Kingore, B. (2004). *Centers in Minutes.* Austin: Professional Associates Publ.

PEG BOARD OR FELT BOARD CENTERS

Cover the back of a piece of furniture with a piece of peg board or felt to gain a potential center. Book shelves also work particularly well for this center conversion.

CENTER-ON-A-SHELF

Plastic bins, pizza boxes, or shirt boxes create centers on a shelf. Label both the container and the designated place on the shelf with the center's name so boxes are easily returned to appropriate places on the shelf. Students select a center box and move to an open floor area to work. When finished, they return the center box to the shelf. (With young children, shirt boxes do not work as well for a long-term center. They are more flimsy and prone to spilling when being carried.)

EXPANDABLE FOLDER CENTERS

Similar to bins or box centers, expandable folders can contain the centers that only require paper and small items, such as centers based upon task cards.

PRIVACY PLACE

Consider providing at least one place that allows privacy for an individual child. This can be accomplished through a big cardboard box that one child might go in or a table cloth extended well over the edges of a table so a child can sit or lay underneath. Some children like to crawl inside spaces and occasionally need the opportunity to choose time alone.

FAST STARTS FOR SUCCESS-FILLED CENTERS

ONE CENTER FIRST

Start simply. Begin with one center to teach the process and behaviors. Add one or more additional centers as you deem that students are ready.

A self-concept center that accents the importance of each person is a success-filled center to begin with because content skills can be less accented. Thus, all students have the opportunity to participate successfully while learning the behaviors and procedures of center time.

ONE LEARNING TASK FIRST

Begin with all students doing the same learning experience at a center until they are sure of the routine. Then, vary the tasks in the center to match the students' range of readiness and diversity of learning profiles.

EACH-ONE-TEACH-ONE

Initially, teach one or two students the most effective procedures and behaviors for centers time. Then, each student teaches another until understanding permeates the entire class.

TRY-OUT TIME

Consider a one-day rotation of only a few minutes at each center for students to *try out* centers and the process of change.

SIMPLE THINGS THAT ADD INTEREST

Little things can add spark to several centers. The following list may prompt brainstroming of other effective choices.

Lamp	Clip boards	Feely box
Flashlight	Sheet (over table)	Stuffed animals
Visor	Tape recorder	Individual chalk-boards
Pillows	Cardboard box	
Sleeping bag	Mirror	Magnifying glass

LONG-TERM CENTERS

Avoid changing centers weekly because of the excessive time involved in that action. Instead, develop centers that are long term. Retain high interest in the centers by adding and deleting only a few items each week or so.

TIME ON TASK

Use learning experiences that require longer thinking time to increase attention spans and encourage high-level-responses. Avoid simple matching tasks or folder games that children complete quickly as that process reinforces short attention spans.

PRE-EXPERIENCED LEARNING TASKS

Mainly use pre-taught products and tasks. If the task has already been modeled with the whole class and successfully applied in small groups, individuals are more likely to experience success without needing assistance. For example, once students have experience with Venn diagrams, they are more likely to be able to complete them using other topics in a center. In general, any learning experience children have successfully experienced in the past becomes a viable task for independent application in a center. (Obviously, the task is varied in its application to retain student enthusiasm.)

STUDENT-CREATED CENTER ORGANIZERS AND GRAPHICS

Involve the students in creating organizational aids for centers. Students feel more ownership in the center when they have assisted in its development. Student-created organizers also save teacher preparation time.

a. Students wrap or decorate cans and box lids for pencil holders and material carryalls.
b, Students write and decorate center signs, labels, and title posters. They can add 3-D items to the posters that are associated with the center, such as pencils and rulers.
c. Students create borders to decorate bulletin boards.

BOOKS AND COMMERCIAL MATERIALS

Review children's literature and commercial task cards to glean ready-to-go center items. Evaluate all types of commercially available materials for those that integrate instruction.

NON-FICTION MATERIALS

Develop centers based upon more non-fiction materials. These materials are easily obtained from school or public library and are preferred by students who want to learn more about subjects of interest, such as dinosaurs, space, and technology.

Kingore, B. (2004). *Centers in Minutes.* Austin: Professional Associates Publ.

STUDENT ASSISTANTS

Use student task assistants and skill assistants to help manage students' questions and needs.

Task Assistants

Task Assistants are students experienced with a specific learning task or product. Working with individuals or small groups, the assistant is recognized as one who can answer questions and provide help when needed. Consider laminating digital photographs of each student to post the current task assistant's picture in a designated place in the classroom. The picture is a positive recognition and informs others of the identity of the assistant. Even students with fewer skills can meet with the teacher in advance to learn how to do a task and then serve as the assistant. All students need multiple opportunities to be task assistants.

Skill Assistants

Skill assistants are students prepared to help others with specific skills. When working with writing conventions, for example, staple different skills (such as the use of commas, capitalization, or specific spelling patterns) to each pocket of a shoe bag or pocket chart. Students write their names on strips cut from index cards and put the name-strips in each specific skill pocket with which they believe they have ample understanding to help others. As students have questions about a skill, they search that skill pocket for the name of a peer available to help. This technique also motivates some students to master a skill as they enjoy being assistants with expertise in that skill.

USE OF MATERIALS

Assist children in the appropriate use of materials as needed. Children need freedom to explore materials in their own way, but they also need some direction when a specific procedure or product is expected. For example, a child who has not used a magnet before and is using it to bang on the table can be shown how the magnet can be used to pick up certain metal objects. A student assistant can remain in a center one day to teach others how to use new materials and equipment.

PLAY VERSUS LEARNING

When presenting new, interesting materials in a center for a first time, allow children to explore and play for awhile before introducing learning task requirements. For example, when children first discover geoboards and rubber bands in a math center they just want to freely explore. After play opportunities, initiate specific geometric patterns you want them to reproduce and you typically find children ready to approach those tasks.

VISUAL APPEAL

Simple graphics can be used all year to add visual appeal and continuity to classroom displays, bulletin boards, and centers. Figures such as the alphabet people and the shape people connect to content priorities in math and language arts with whimsical appeal. They can be used as borders and decorative accents.

Kingore, B. (2004). *Centers in Minutes.* Austin: Professional Associates Publ.

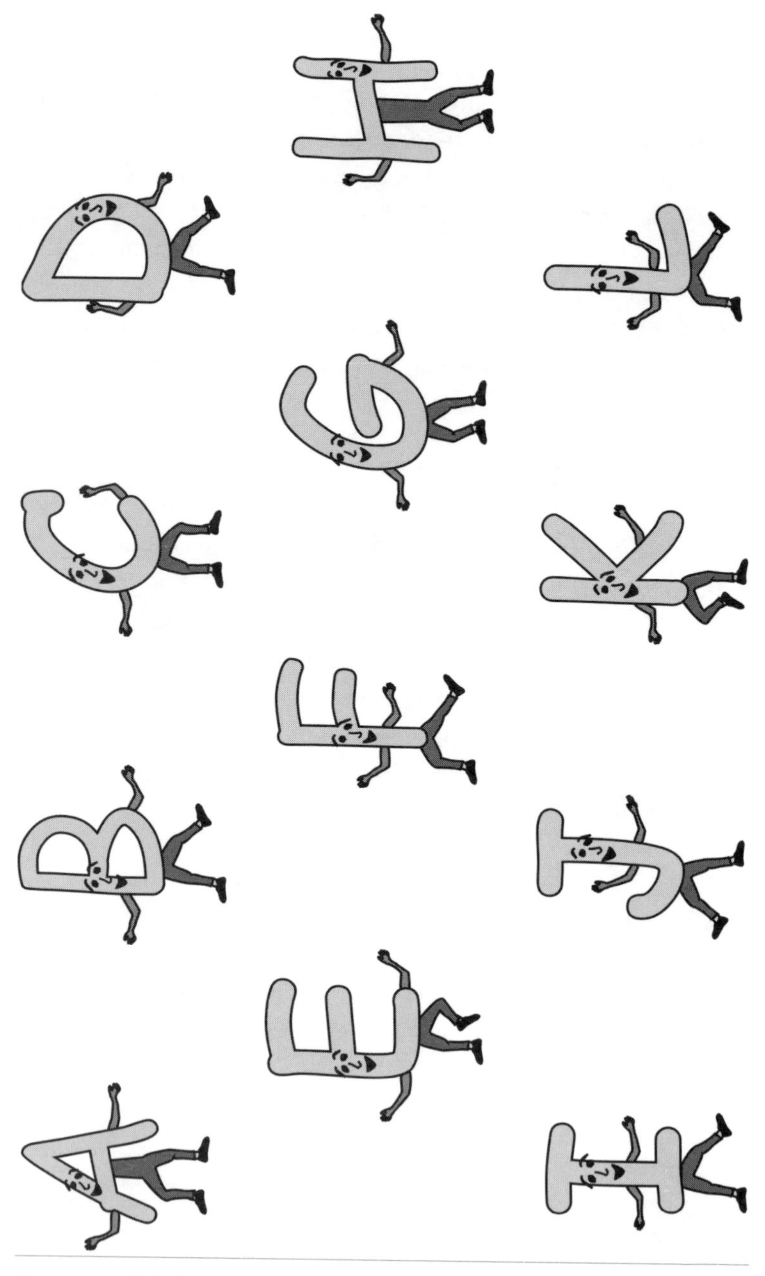

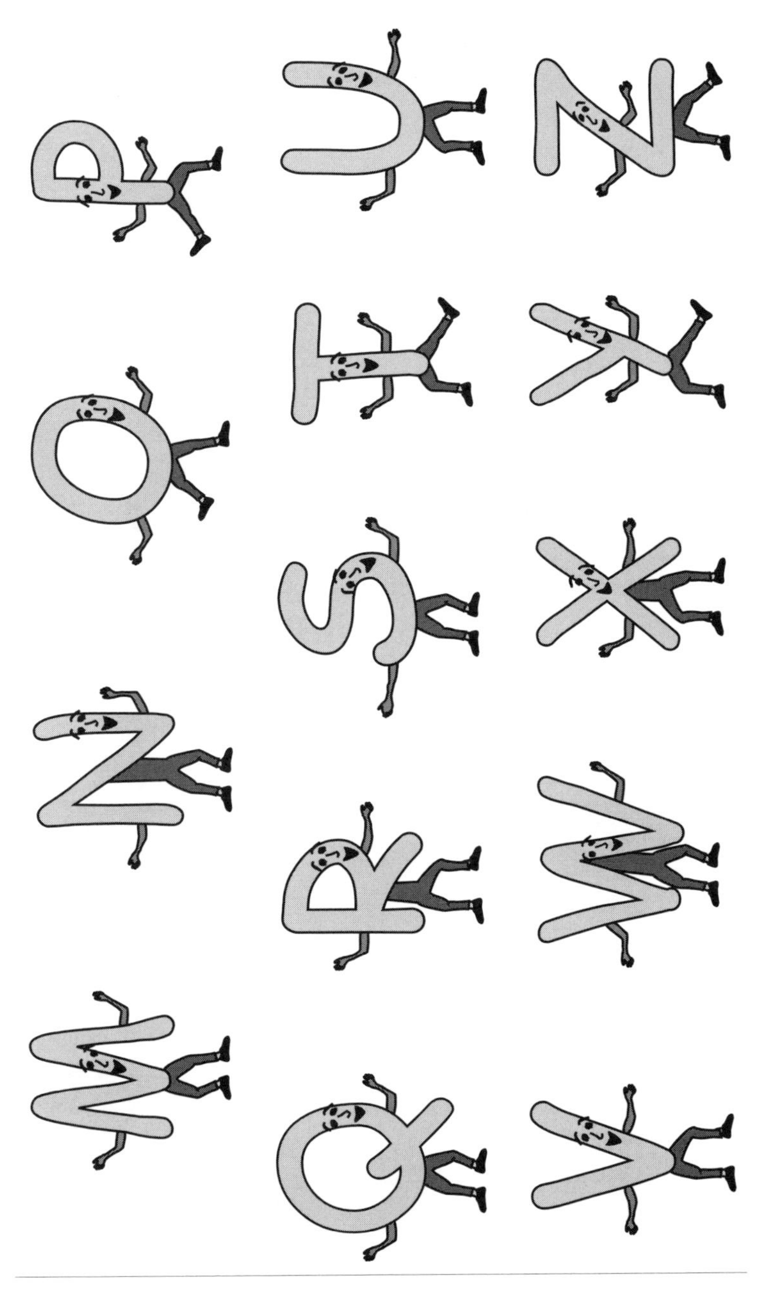

Kingore, B. (2004). *Centers in Minutes.* Austin: Professional Associates Publ.

Kingore, B. (2004). *Centers in Minutes.* Austin: Professional Associates Publ.

ORGANIZING CENTERS

Provide the appropriate number and kind of centers for your room size, arrangement, and number of students.

HOW MANY STUDENTS SHOULD BE IN A CENTER?

Determine how many students can work productively at a center at the same time, and how many students the center space and materials accommodate. For example, if there are three computers, the center serves three students or less. If there is space at a writing center for four chairs, then four students could be involved. Generally, a smaller number of

---

Kingore, B. (2004). *Centers in Minutes.* Austin: Professional Associates Publ.

students at a center enables quieter productivity. Hence, three or four is better than six.

When space and equipment allow, the simplest process is to have the same number of children in each center, such as four per center. This system is easy to remember.

HOW MANY CENTERS ARE NEEDED?

$$\text{\# of centers} = \frac{\text{the total \# of students at all of the centers}}{\text{the \# of students preferred at each center}}$$

If all students are at centers at the same time, centers must have room for the total number of students plus two or three extra spaces to allow choice and change. In other words, in a class of 26 children, approximately 28 center spaces are needed. If four students are to be in a center at one time, then seven centers would be needed.

Students are not necessarily all in centers at the same time. For example, some students might work with the teacher as others work independently at their seats and others are in centers. In a room of 27 children, if one-third of the students are in centers at a time, spaces for nine children are needed. In this case, only three centers with three or four students in each are required. Provide room for the number of students who will be at each center at one time plus an extra space or two if changing centers is allowed.

CENTER MODELS

THE TEACHER DIRECTS ONE GROUP

1. One-Third Model

One-third of the class works with the teacher in a guided learning group, one-third works completing independent work, and one-third works in centers. Therefore, only enough center places for one-third of the class is required at a time. Centers, independent work, and guided instruction with the teacher are completed in a one and one-half hour block of time with students rotating among the options. All students participate in all three learning formats each day.

2. Four Centers Daily Rotation

There are four centers in the room, one of which is guided by the teacher. All students rotate through all centers each day. Center time runs for one hour with 15 minutes per center, or one hour and 20 minutes with 20 minutes per center.

3. Open-Choice Model

Centers are established on the planning board. During centers time, students select among the centers to enable them to complete a certain number by the end of one or two weeks. As students work in centers, the teacher selects groups of students to work with in a guided lesson. Depending on time, the teacher works with each group each day or two or three times a week. Center time runs from 45 minutes to one hour or more.

Kingore, B. (2004). *Centers in Minutes.* Austin: Professional Associates Publ.

TEACHER FACILITATES ALL GROUPS IN CENTERS

1. Variation of Open-choice Model

Centers are established on the planning board and students select among the centers to complete a certain number by the end of one or two weeks. As students work in centers, the teacher facilitates and assesses students' strengths and needs. Center time runs for 45 minutes.

2. One-Center-a-Day Rotation

Five centers are used all week and students are placed in five groups that participate in centers at the same time. Provide enough places at each center to accommodate 1/5 of the total class. Center time runs for 20-30 minutes. Each day, a group rotates to a different center so that by the end of the week, all five centers have been visited by each student. The teacher facilitates and assesses during center time.

ORGANIZING STUDENTS INTO CENTERS

There are many ways to direct children to learning centers. Avoid beginning the week with explanations in which the students sit and watch as the teacher goes around the centers, providing all of the needed information. This practice takes too long, and children tune out. It is a less effective learning model because there is no real involvement in learning by the children. Such lengthy interactions are not needed if centers mainly integrate previously taught activities and use children as center assistants.

MORNING MEETINGS WITH CHILDREN'S NAME STICKS OR LOLLIPOPS

At the closure of the morning group time, the teacher or a child randomly selects students' name sticks or lollipops-- a popcycle stick with a child's name printed on it or on a construction paper circle attached to it. As each name is drawn, that child chooses a center and places the name stick in a decorated container in the center. That center is open until the designated number of students' names are in the container.

The random nature of drawing names makes this method seem equitable. However, techniques for students' record keeping (discussed later in this book) should be added to this method to prevent students from overusing the same centers. Furthermore, this method requires several minutes to get students settled into centers. Some time is wasted as children just look around to make a decision.

ROTATION POSTERS

Rotation methods have the greatest teacher control. The teacher assigns students to groups based upon mixed-readiness, similar readiness, or interests. Choice is provided by the activity variety within each center.

The groups rotate among the centers in a predetermined sequence at teacher-directed times. Cards with groups of students' names are placed on a poster to designate in which center each group is to begin working. For example, children review a merry-go-round poster to see which center their group is assigned. Every day, a different center is assigned so that after a few days, all centers have been visited by all of the children. Change the groupings frequently to enable different children to experience working with each other.

CONTRACTS

Self-motivated students with independent skills can contract which centers they want to or need to complete. The teacher and student meet briefly to complete the contract and agree upon centers according to the child's assessed needs and readiness levels. (Examples of student contracts are shared in the student record keeping section of this book.) Contracting increases student responsibilities and lessens direct teacher control.

Kingore, B. (2004). *Centers in Minutes.* Austin: Professional Associates Publ.

OPEN-CHOICE PLANNING BOARD

A planning board displays an icon for each center in the room. Under each icon is a short length of wide yarn with clothespins attached. The number of clothespins designates the number of children who can work in that center at one time. Each icon is glued on a different color of paper and the clothespins under each are spray painted to match that color.

Students go to the planning board and select the center in which they want to work. They then attach the corresponding clothespin to their clothing. The color makes it easy to identify which students are supposed to be in that center.

When children complete the center, they return the clothespin to the planning board, and select another center. This method encourages more responsibility and flexibility. Teachers report less discipline problems as students chose their own place and pacing. This method eliminates the problem of some children finishing earlier than others.

As a variation, a planning board can also be made with center icons and a hook for laminated paper keys below each. Students' names are on the keys. The students hang their name key under the icon to select a center. Teachers can write a number beside each center icon to denote how many may be in that center.

Providing choice is like having a learning environment barometer-- students' choices document which centers and tasks best match children's needs and interests.

Kingore, B. (2004). *Centers in Minutes.* Austin: Professional Associates Publ.

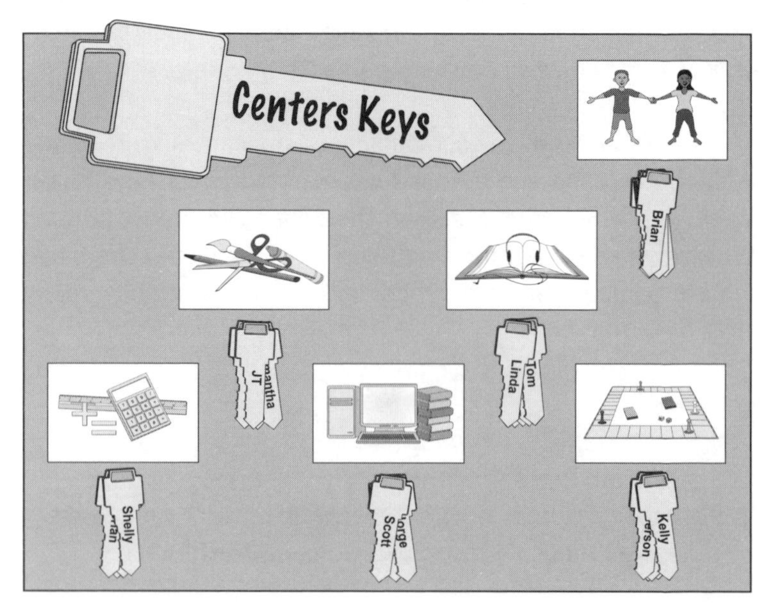

Kingore, B. (2004). *Centers in Minutes.* Austin: Professional Associates Publ.

COMBINATIONS OVER TIME

Over time, combinations of the different methods may prove useful. For example, a teacher might begin with the control of teacher-directed rotation in order to model centers and provide time for students to increase their self-management skills. Later, the teacher can initiate an open-choice planning board and student recording keeping to increase students' responsibilities and independence.

CENTERS ICONS

Icons that represent different centers are an effective communication device. Use them to organize centers and simplify record keeping. Provide copes of the icons for students to cut out as needed in order to complete their centers logs, tickets, or calenders.

Actors' Place

Children explore with simple props for role playing scenarios such as a home, doctor's office, store, bank, and post office.

Artists' Studio

Creative visual arts such as drawing, painting, sketching, and cut paper are encouraged in this center.

Computer Lab

Writers use the computers to complete compositions while others use the software programs related to content areas.

Kingore, B. (2004). *Centers in Minutes.* Austin: Professional Associates Publ.

Construction Zone

A variety of manipulatives including blocks and legos are available for building and problem solving.

Mathematical Thinking

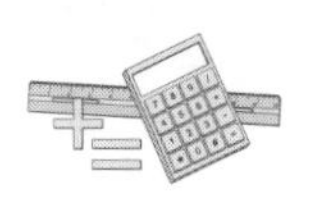

Math manipulatives are provided for students to solve math problems, create graphs, and explore relationships.

Overhead Projector

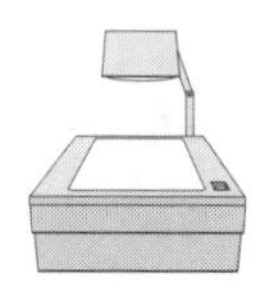

The overhead invites children to practice writing and fine-motor tasks on an overhead transparency and then project their work onto a chalkboard to trace using large muscles.

Portfolio Center

This center includes all of the materials, forms, and hanging files students need to organize products for their portfolios.

Read and Listen

A wide range of literature, both fiction and nonfiction, is available for children's reading or listening delight.

Research Center

A computer and multiple resources encourage children to seek more information about their favorite topics. The materials reflect students' specific interests.

Kingore, B. (2004). *Centers in Minutes.* Austin: Professional Associates Publ.

Science Lab

Scientific explorations are provided here with equipment and problem-solving tasks for scientists to observe, predict, record, and write.

Sounds of Music

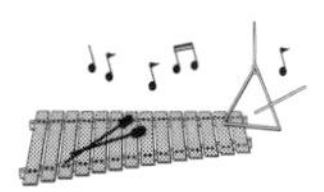

A range of musical instruments and instructions for creating instruments are provided with song books and tape recorders.

Strategy Center

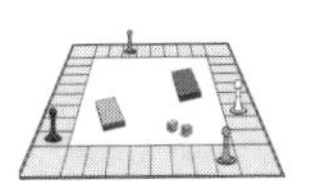

This center contains a collection of board and strategy games that children play to apply thinking and communication skills.

Thinking About Me

This place is a celebration of self. Students complete interest surveys, family records, and illustrate what is important to them.

Wonderful Words

Intriguing challenges with letters and words invite children to use a variety of games, strategies, and reference materials.

A World of People

Children investigate social studies connections involving maps, cultures, and lifestyles of the past, present, and future.

Write On!

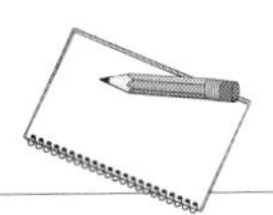

Writing tools, colored paper, unexpected items, and sources of print invite children to be authors.

Kingore, B. (2004). *Centers in Minutes.* Austin: Professional Associates Publ.

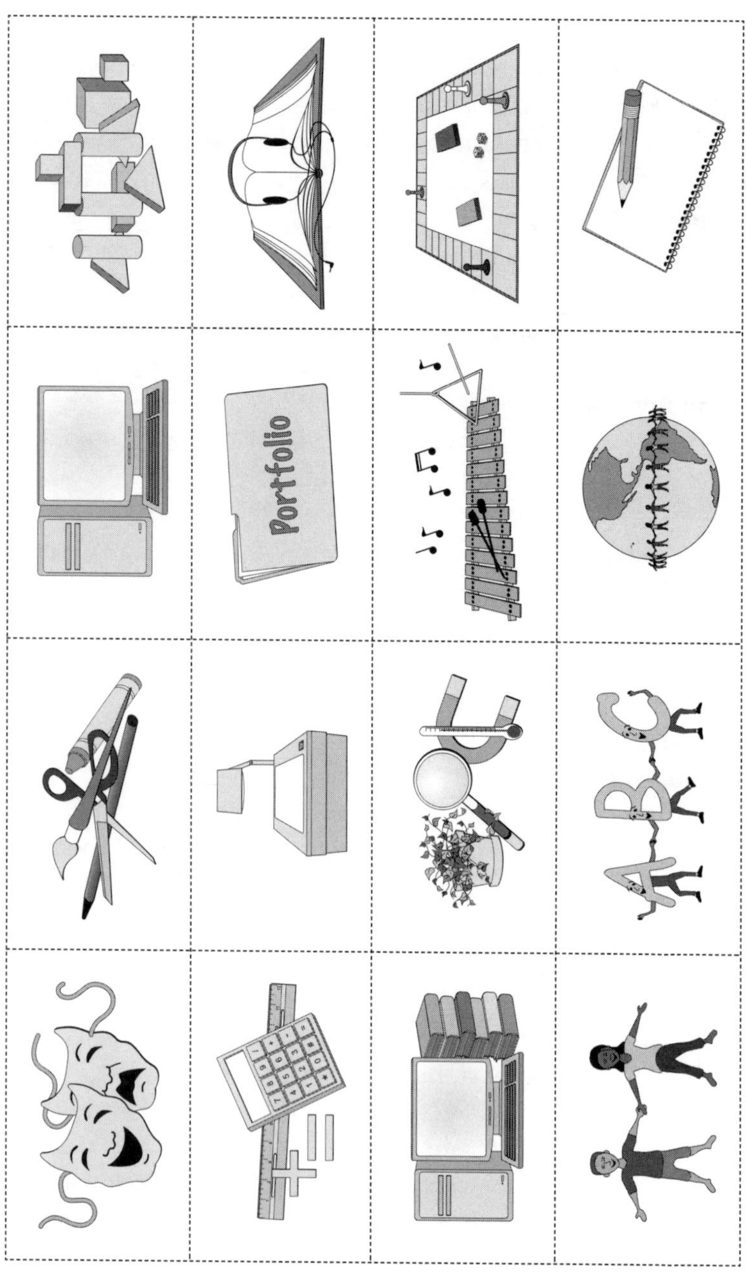

Kingore, B. (2004). *Centers in Minutes.* Austin: Professional Associates Publ.

PREPARING STUDENTS FOR CENTERS

Before initiating centers, prepare students with the parameters of the task so they know what is expected and which behaviors are desired. The following suggestions help prepare students for successful outcomes.

- ✔ Model and teach children how to use centers and materials constructively.

- ✔ Involve students in role playing the process, such as working quietly, cleaning up, and displaying work. Children experience significantly less behavior management problems when they have participated in practice sessions with role play. Have them literally walk through a simulation of how to clean up and move to the next center.

Kingore, B. (2004). *Centers in Minutes.* Austin: Professional Associates Publ.

✔ As an engaging switch, the teacher role plays a student working in centers. The students watch and offer suggestions to improve what is being done incorrectly.

✔ When difficulties occur, incorporate a brief mini-lesson and problem-solve with the class ways to resolve the conflict.

Mini-Lesson Topics
Using the Planning Board
Working quietly
Using materials or equipment correctly
Moving from center to center
Reorganizing when center time ends
Getting needed materials
Posting work on a board
Cooperating with others in centers
Completing self-assessments accurately
Record keeping (Centers Logs)
Interacting with task or skill assistants
Responding to signals

✔ Use learning tasks that students have experienced successfully. When they already know how to complete a task, following the directions independently is easier.

✔ Provide clearly developed directions, criteria, and expectations before the center begins.
- Provide verbal and written directions to eliminate confusion and reach diverse learning modalities.
- Discuss the expectations for centers. Then, post a rubric that clarifies quality and behaviors.

POSITIVE WORK BEHAVIORS

Work with students to develop a list of the behaviors that children can and should practice to promote their responsibility for learning and to develop their independent learning skills. Students feel more ownership when they participate in the process of establishing classroom expectations. State the behaviors in positive terms as much as possible, communicating what to do rather than what not to do. Furthermore, less may be best. Keep the list as brief as is appropriate to students' needs. Post these behaviors in the classroom and share them with parents.

The next page provides several questions posed to help focus and establish positive work behaviors in the classroom, particularly when the teacher is occupied instructing other students. The time spent developing positive work behaviors can result in increased student task-commitment and production.

Clarify which behaviors are nonnegotiable. For example, it is not debatable *if* clean up will occur, only *how* it will be completed. Once your priorities are determined, guide students in a discussion of work behavior parameters. Developing positive work behaviors with students avoids many potential behavior problems.

Students who feel ownership in establishing classroom expectations are more likely to be responsible learners.

Establishing a Positive Learning Environment for Centers

- ❖ How many students may work together in a center?
- ❖ Which combinations of the following enable the most effective initial instruction?
    - Whole-class oral instructions
    - Posted written instructions
    - Rebus charts and instructions
    - Audiotaped instructions
    - Individuals or small groups meetings
    - Student Assistants
- ❖ What are the guidelines for noise levels?
- ❖ What are students to do when they need supplies or materials?
- ❖ What combination of options are available when help is needed for students working independently?
    - Peer collaboration
    - Student Assistants
    - Adult assistance in room from parents or teaching assistants
- ❖ What are students to do with completed products?
- ❖ What are students to do with work-in-progress that will be continued in the next class period?
- ❖ What clean up and reorganization responsibilities are required?
- ❖ What opportunities are provided for students to share ideas and work with others?
    - Sharing time after centers or at the end of the day
    - Board to post work for others to read and respond
    - Student-written letters to parents about centers

Kingore, B. (2004). *Centers in Minutes.* Austin: Professional Associates Publ.

DEFINING QUALITY

Teach students to work toward quality. In past learning environments, students may have misconstrued that being correct, neat, and on time were the valued criteria. Guide students to understand that those attributes are important, but that quality is the target. Class time spent discussing and defining quality can increase students' commitment to excellence.

✔ Show examples of high-quality and lower-quality products to help students form more concrete targets.

✔ As a class, develop a rubric for quality. A rubric can communicate the desired working behaviors and levels of achievements. For example, the rubric might progress from *accurate information,* to *thoughtful information and details,* to *in-depth, clearly supported information.*

✔ Establish a reason for quality by announcing to students how their work will be shared. Examples of several options follow.

- Post the work on a board for others to view.
- Demonstrate the process or share the work with a younger student.
- Share the work orally during class discussions.
- Discuss the work with one to three classmates in a group for peer response. *Tell each other one thing you did well in centers today.*
- Share products with someone at home. Requesting a brief written response from whomever reviews the work may add even more importance and long-term enjoyment to the process.

INITIATING NOISE CONTROL

✔ Concretely establish the desired range of volume. As a class, discuss a *productive buzz* of sound versus the roar of *chaos*. Role play the different levels of sound on a continuum from *preferred* to *out of control*. Noise problems tend to reoccur, so be prepared to revisit earlier discussions and role play again.

✔ Elicit students' ideas. Students may have more ownership in noise control efforts when they participate in establishing the parameters.

✔ Talk softly as much as possible. A soft voice often makes students listen more carefully. Conversely, as you increase your volume, so do others in the room.

SIGNALS AND CENTERS TRANSITIONS

Children do not change gears effortlessly. They need to be informed ahead of time that it is almost time to change so they can bring closure to their current task. Use signals that inform students when to begin and end tasks. Once established, signals save class time because fewer directions need to be verbalized. They are one factor that produces smoother, more quiet transitions.

Establish a signal for the class to be quiet. As a class, determine a simple signal to use when immediate attention or quiet is needed, such as when an announcement is made or a refocus is required. Examples of effective signals include: ringing a bell, hands raised and held in place, clap patterns, and verbal statements, such as: *When you hear my voice, snap* [fingers snap one time]. Each signal is held or repeated until the desired level of quiet is reached.

Use signals to guide students' time management. Different signals can be used to represent different messages. For example, three claps can mean three minutes remain. If a signal begins to lose its value, more inventive signals should be substituted, such as an ah-ooga horn, whistle, or musical chord.

Signal a three-minute warning to prepare students by letting them know the limited time remaining. This signal informs children that it is time to reach closure with their activities and clean up. Three minutes later, follow with a transition signal for students to rotate to another center or conclude center time.

When center time concludes, begin a transition activity that is interesting enough most students immediately want to participate. Student-directed activities work especially well for this time so the teacher is free to facilitate and oversee the closure of center activities.

SIGNAL EXAMPLES

1. ***Lights***
   Flash them on and off.

2. ***Sound***
   Consider using a xylophone run, bell, clap pattern, an ah-ooga horn, whistle, or musical chord. (Vocal sounds are least effective).

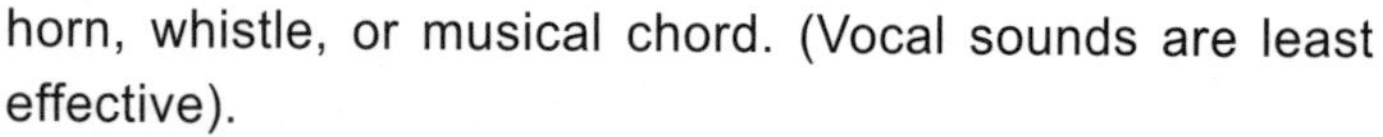

3. ***Musical Tapes or CDs***
   Some teachers use a remote control to activate a CD of music that is established as the signal piece. The same musical selection is used repeatedly so students know: *When you hear the music...*

   Plan a three-minute segment of the music. When it begins to play, children are to begin cleaning up and reorganizing the center. As children become familiar with the segment, they learn to pace their concluding tasks so they finish as the music ends.

   Consider using classical selections for this transition to expose children to a wider variety of music. Remember that the brain research indicates classical music with its more complex structures, especially the compositions of Mozart and Bach, helps to increase brain activity. Change the selection monthly so children are exposed to many different compositions.

4. ***Announce and Pause***
   Announce the behavior and then tell students when to proceed. This signal gives students a second to process the information before acting upon it. *In two seconds, you may quietly move to your center. (Pause.) Begin.*

5. ***Countdown***
   In primary classrooms, teachers lead students in an oral countdown as a beginning and ending: *10, 9, 8, 7, 6...*

6. ***Chant***
   When students rotate among tasks or centers, teachers can use the simple chant: *2-4-6-8, rotate.*

7. ***Debriefing***
   For the last two minutes of a center, initiate debriefing and closure among the students at that center. *Tell one person at the center about something you worked on or completed today. (Pause) Now, switch parts.*

8. ***Transition Songs***
   Create transition songs by substituting information messages as the words to well-know tunes.

   - Transition for center rotations:
     (TUNE: "Mulberry Bush" - When time for rotation)
     ROUND AND ROUND THE CENTERS WE GO.
     IT'S TIME TO MOVE TO THE NEXT IN THE ROW.

Kingore, B. (2004). *Centers in Minutes.* Austin: Professional Associates Publ.

- Transition for ending center time:
  (TUNE: "Mulberry Bush" - Three minutes before end of centers)
  IT'S TIME TO PUT THE CENTERS AWAY,
  CENTERS AWAY, CENTERS AWAY.
  IT'S TIME TO PUT THE CENTERS AWAY,
  WE'LL WORK IN THEM ANOTHER DAY.

PARENT COMMUNICATION

It is beneficial to inform parents about the objectives and values of centers through newsletters and an evening workshop for them. Parents are more likely to appreciate what their child is learning when they understand the value of learning centers.

Consider, at a parent night at school, asking parents to complete a skill sheet and then interact in a center using the same skills. Elicit their response regarding mental engagement and transfer potential of the two experiences. Many parents understand the value of centers better after this experience! Share your rubrics for quality and learning standards integrations with parents to help them realize the value of centers specific to students needs and learning objectives.

Kingore, B. (2004). *Centers in Minutes.* Austin: Professional Associates Publ.

As an authentic writing task, have children write a letter to their parent describing a center that they enjoy. Ensure that the children explain how the specific center is important and what they are learning during center time.

Teachers can also send letters to parents to explain the purposes of centers and clarify the learning that is promoted. A sample letter to parents follows.

Dear ________________________,

Your child participates in learning centers as one important part of learning in our class. Learning centers are more than an interactive way to learn. They allow a variety of learning experiences that draw on diverse learning strengths and interests to ensure that all childrne have multiple ways to experience continued learning success. They are a significant part of our objective to provide opportunities for children to experience responsibility, decision-making, cooperation, and self-assessment.

Your child is able to explain our learning centers to you and is eager to share them with you as you have an opportunity to visit our classroom. Notice the skills listed in each center to help you understand what your child is learning.

If you have questions or concerns about anything you see or hear, please write or call me so we can discuss them together. Thank you for participating in your child's education.

Sincerely,

Kingore, B. (2004). *Centers in Minutes.* Austin: Professional Associates Publ.

TEACHERS' ROLES

Teachers have many different roles during centers. The following are possibilities to consider.

a. Facilitate and assess students' work during center time when all children are participating in centers at the same time. Conversations among children in centers provide many assessment opportunities and reveal the process as well as the products of learning. Listening to what children say as they work provides insight into their schema and level of achievement. Many teachers determine extension or reteaching needs from assessments during centers.

   Writing notes while moving among the groups piques students' self-awareness. Students may ask: *What*

Kingore, B. (2004). *Centers in Minutes.* Austin: Professional Associates Publ.

are you writing. My most effective response is: *Things I need to remember about your work.* Students are not exactly sure what that means and usually get back on task quickly.

Accent teacher proximity. Move near groups who need a reminder or refocus.

b. Work with one small group of students, guiding their instruction as the rest of the children participate in centers. As needed, write quick notes of problems to address with other groups when finished directly teaching the current group. Recording the problem for later action prevents an interruption to instruction and saves the valuable time of the group with whom you are working.

c. Conference and problem solve with specific students as the rest of the children participate in centers. Large numbers of mini-conferences can be accomplished in this manner. Arrange "appointments" with students before center time to avoid a student being in a center and not wanting to or not being able to stop.

d. Combine the above roles.

e. Help a child who is having trouble entering into a group's activity by establishing an assignment or needed role for them to assume. For example, during role play in Actor's Place, introduce the child as someone who has come to visit.

STUDENTS' RECORD KEEPING

CENTERS LOG

Promote students' record keeping through centers logs in which they record the tasks they engage in and self-assess the quality of their work. Much of the record keeping responsibilities in centers can and should be completed by students. Centers logs enable students and teachers to easily track what has been accomplished and which centers need to be completed next. Each log contains one copy of the title and rubric card with multiple copies of the third card to respond to multiple centers.

Using the Centers Logs on the following pages, students can cut out and staple together a booklet in which they

---

Kingore, B. (2004). *Centers in Minutes.* Austin: Professional Associates Publ.

record their daily centers work. One log has less writing required for young students who simply cut and paste the picture of the center they worked in and draw the face they earned for the quality of work they completed. The second log requires students to write what they did in the center and what they learned. They also record the grade they earned according to the rubric.

CENTERS TICKET

Provide each student with a copy of the Centers Ticket. After completing a center, students paste the corresponding icon onto the ticket. They then self-evaluate by drawing beside the center name the face or grade they earned for their work. The intent is for children to complete all centers one time before they repeat working in a center.

CENTERS CALENDAR

Another option for young children is to provide a Centers Calendar for the week. Students cut out and glue in each date the icon for the center they completed that day.

CONTRACTS

Students complete a contract to record their center choices and what they will accomplish. The teacher meets briefly with a student to initiate the contract and assign some activities or centers according to the child's assessed needs and readiness level. Contracts can also be used for students to commit to the positive work behaviors they will practice during center time.

Thinking in Progress!

NAME ______________________________
I did this today:

This is my next step:

THINKING IN PROGRESS

Some students may not complete a center in a single visit because of difficulties they experience or because they are embellishing and developing their product with depth. Provide copies of a Thinking in Progress slip that students complete and post with their work as a status note.

PORTFOLIOS

The products children produce in centers are authentic indicators of their interests and abilities. When students' organization, problem solving, and self-assessments are incorporated in a center, the collection of student products evolves into a portfolio that more authentically documents growth and achievement levels than traditional assessment procedures alone.*

*Kingore, B. (1999). *Assessment: Time-Saving Procedures for Busy Teachers,* 2nd ed. Austin: Professional Associates Publishing.

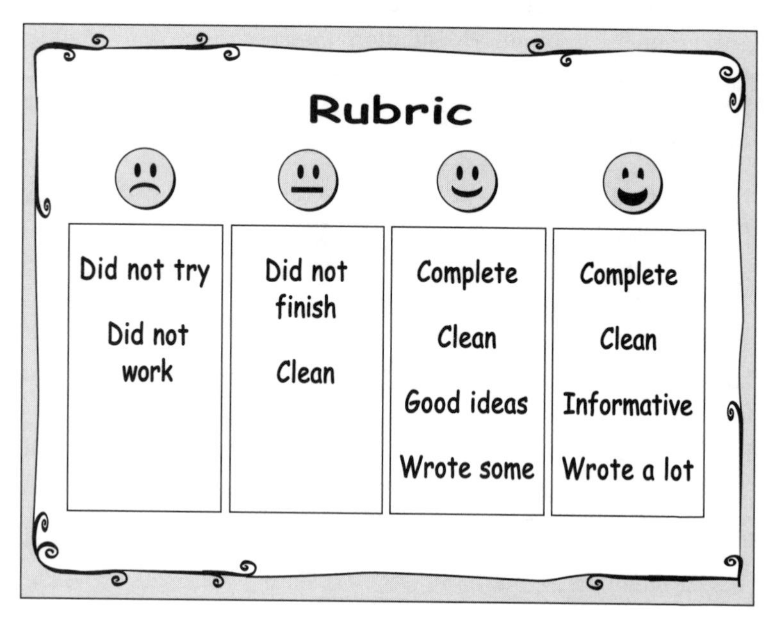

Kingore, B. (2004). *Centers in Minutes.* Austin: Professional Associates Publ.

Kingore, B. (2004). *Centers in Minutes.* Austin: Professional Associates Publ.

Rubric

A

My work is complete and carefully done.
I used original ideas.
I encouraged and helped others.
I helped clean.
My work is well developed, detailed, interesting, and uses precise vocabulary.

B

My work is complete.
I used only my own ideas.
I helped others.
I helped clean.
My work is accurate, informative, and detailed.

C

I worked but did not finish.
I used some of my own ideas.
I tried to help.
I helped clean.
My work has accurate information.

Below Standard

I did not follow the directions. I did not work.

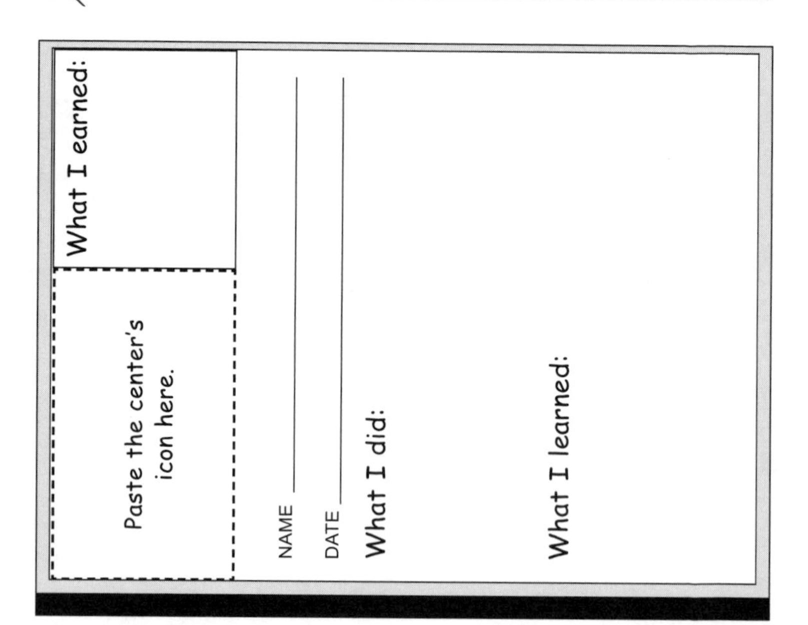

What I earned:

Paste the center's icon here.

NAME ____________

DATE ____________

What I did:

What I learned:

Kingore, B. (2004). *Centers in Minutes.* Austin: Professional Associates Publ.

Centers Ticket

NAME ________________________________

DATE ________________________________

Paste the center's icon here.

Paste the center's icon here.

Paste the center's icon here.

Paste the center's icon here.

Kingore, B. (2004). *Centers in Minutes.* Austin: Professional Associates Publ.

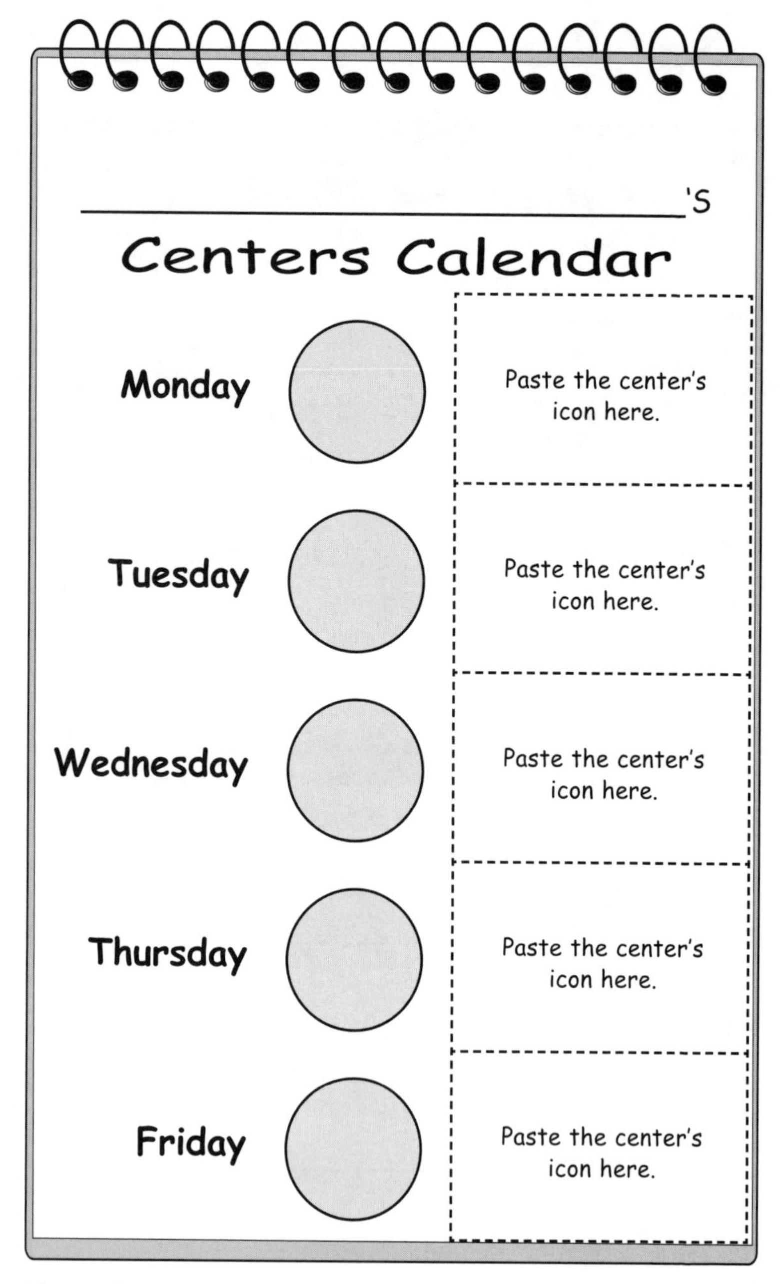
_______________'s
Centers Calendar
Monday
Paste the center's icon here.
Tuesday
Paste the center's icon here.
Wednesday
Paste the center's icon here.
Thursday
Paste the center's icon here.
Friday
Paste the center's icon here.

Learning Centers Contract

BEGINNING ________________ ENDING ________________

I selected
these centers:

Paste the center's
icon here.

Paste the center's
icon here.

I will work:

- ❑ During centers time.
- ❑ When I compact out of ________________.

POSITIVE WORK BEHAVIORS
I will do all I can to help myself and others learn.

I will self-assess daily in my centers log.

My teacher will check my work:

- ❑ As I finish each activity.
- ❑ Once each week.
- ❑ During our conference on: ________________

My teacher
selected this center:

Paste the center's
icon here.

STUDENT ________________________________

TEACHER ________________________________

Kingore, B. (2004). *Centers in Minutes.* Austin: Professional Associates Publ.

Contract for Positive Work Behaviors

- ❑ I will stay on task and manage my time.
- ❑ I will carefully finish my work.
- ❑ I will work with others quietly.
- ❑ I will respect the property of others.
- ❑ I will do everything I can to help myself and others learn.
- ❑ I will self-assess my work process and product.
- ❑ I will place completed work in the place designated by my teacher.
- ❑ I will reorganize and return all materials and resources in the center when I finish.
- ❑ ______________________________
  ____
- ❑ ______________________________
  ____

I will follow these guidelines as I work in centers.

STUDENT ______________________________

TEACHER ______________________ DATE ______________

COMMON PROBLEMS AND POSSIBLE SOLUTIONS

As a general rule, reason in reverse. Predict potential problems and then brainstorm how to prevent them.

1. The time and energy it takes to develop centers

SOLUTIONS:

- *Centers in minutes*--Create centers that minimize preparation time and maximize students' interactive learning. Switch the focus from *beautiful centers* to simple centers with learning opportunities that are *beautiful* because of their educational value.
- Involve students more in producing parts of centers, such as signs and organizational devices.

Kingore, B. (2004). *Centers in Minutes.* Austin: Professional Associates Publ.

2. Centers that are "fluff" instead of instructionally vibrant--centers that only keep kids busy or entertain them.

SOLUTION:

Children deserve to learn and there are numerous concepts and skills they need to learn. Integrate standards into each center that incorporate the essential outcomes or skills for the grade level.

3. Adults who do not understand the value of centers

SOLUTIONS:

- Post learning standards in each center so everyone can see the learning connections incorporated into the center tasks.
- Provide information to parents regarding the educational value of centers.

4. Students hurrying through their regular work to get to centers more quickly

SOLUTIONS:

- Post a rubric clarifying the quality that is expected in regular work and in centers.
- Require students to self-assess and reflect on their accomplishments. Conduct brief, private discussions with students who do not self-assess accurately.
- Require the completion of quality work. Students who abuse that lose their privilege of choice.

As long as you complete required work
at an appropriate quality level, you determine
when you are ready to go to centers.
If not completing quality work,
you lose the privaledge of determining
when you go to centers. Then, I must first review
your completed work before you enter centers.

5. Students playing around in centers instead of working and being productive

SOLUTIONS:

- Post a chart of positive work behaviors.
- Incorporate a rubric defining quality work.
- Require students to self-assess and reflect on their accomplishments. A center log is a simple device for organizing this reflection.
- Allow a smaller number of students in a center.

6. Students interrupting when the teacher is directing other children in a small group

SOLUTIONS:

- Discuss with the class your needs as their teacher and the importance of respecting others' right to learn.
- Incorporate a visual signal informing students that you may not be interrupted. Signals that other teachers have successfully used include a tiara, a Do Not Disturb sign hung around the neck, and a desert island graphic in a stand-up picture frame.
- Provide student assistants for tasks and skills.

7. Centers left in a disarray because students do not clean up the area

SOLUTIONS:

- Post positive work behaviors
- Signal a two or three minute warning. That signal prepares students by letting them know the limited time remaining. After the two or three minutes, follow with a transition signal for students to rotate to another center or conclude center time.
- Practice preventative management by pre-planning to

---

avoid messes. For example, place a bucket containing a few inches of water and small sponges beside an art easel. Children simply wipe off the easel each time they paint. (Some students enjoy the water play as much as the painting.)

8. Students who never get to be in centers because their other work is not finished quickly enough

SOLUTIONS:

- Avoid using centers only as alternatives for students who finish early.
- Incorporate a rotation system. As long as students are responsible and working, they move into centers when it is their time.
- Evaluate independent work. Ensure that it is the appropriate tier of challenge for each student. Students who are frustrated or overwhelmed need intervention and task accommodation.

9. Students who finish center work before time to change centers

SOLUTIONS:

- Provide one extra center: *Extra! Extra! Learn All About It!* Children who complete quality work at an assigned center can go to the extra center containing a potpourri of thinking, art, or problem-solving activities that are easy to add to and change.
- Use an open-choice planning board that allows children to change centers as they complete tasks rather than on a schedule.

Index

CD-ROM

Centers in Minutes, Volume 1

Dr. Bertie Kingore

ID CODE: BK-08 $9.95
Grades: K - 8

Interactive CD-ROM

This CD-ROM is the companion to *Centers in Minutes!* It includes illustrations and patterns in color and in multiple sizes. Also included are directions for organizing specific centers PREPARED IN MINUTES, such as: A Strategy Center, Recording Studio, Write On, Read and Listen, Portfolio Center, and two centers based upon children's literature.

Current Publications by
Bertie Kingore, Ph.D.

Alphabetters: Thinking Adventures with the Alphabet (Task Cards)
Assessment: Time Saving Procedures for Busy Teachers, 2nd ed.
Differentiation: Simplified, Realistic, and Effective
Engaging Creative Thinking: Activities to Integrate Creative Problem Solving
Integrating Thinking: Practical Strategies and Activities to Encourage High-Level Responses
Just What I Need! Learning Experiences to Use on Multiple Days in Multiple Ways
Kingore Observation Inventory (KOI), 2nd ed.
Literature Celebrations: Catalysts for High-Level Book Responses, 2nd ed.
Portfolios: Enriching and Assessing All Students; Identifying the Gifted, Grades K-6
Reading Strategies for Advanced Primary Readers: Texas Reading Initiative Task Force for the Education of Primary Gifted Children
Reading Strategies for Advanced Primary Readers: Professional Development Guide
Rubrics and More! The Assessment Companion
Teaching Without Nonsense: Activities to Encourage High-Level Responses
We Care: A Curriculum for Preschool Through Kindergarten, 2nd ed.